4 Seasons Life
IN NEW HAMPSHIRE

WMUR-TV 9

Published by Pediment Publishing, a division of The Pediment Group, Inc. www.pediment.com Printed in Canada

Table of Contents

Foreword

Each season in New Hampshire brings different opportunities to enjoy all the Granite State has to offer. The photos in this book and on the enclosed DVD are a testament to both the state's natural beauty and the quality of life in New Hampshire.

Moreover, this book is only possible thanks to the tens of thousands of members of WMUR's ulocal community who sent in over 80,000 pictures of winter, spring, summer and fall.

In the spirit of so many sharing so much, we again believe it fitting to donate a portion of the proceeds from this project to an organization helping those who desperately need it: The New Hampshire Food Bank. They are the largest non-profit food distribution center in the state, and through their agencies provide meals and assistance to over 125,000 people each year.

For this project, photos were considered regardless of when they were taken, so long as they were taken in New Hampshire. A few from seasons long ago have been included to show the timelessness of our state. We hope you enjoy this collection of user photographs celebrating 4 Seasons - Life in New Hampshire.

WINTER

WAITING FOR SUMMER IN NH *(previous top left):* This photo was taken a few days after a snowstorm. The motivation for taking this shot was that it actually looked like the chairs were longing for warmer weather. ⓟ (DavePaquin)

WINTERSCAPE *(previous top middle):* I woke up this morning and looked out my window. The sunrise was just beautiful, causing the trees to look like it was fall again. ⓟ (fanof34)

DYLAN CATCHES A SNOWFLAKE *(previous top right):* ⓟ Lorraine Aucoin (aucelk)

MAKING THE TURN *(previous middle left):* ⓟ (davefar)

OUR CHRISTMAS TREE *(previous middle right):* ⓟ Brenda T. Drew (BTDREW)

TEMPLE NH SLEIGH RIDE *(previous bottom left):* The minis are named Mighty and Fancy. The horse is Annie. ⓟ (drdave)

ICE STORM *(previous bottom middle):* ⓟ (Trier)

KIDS ON A ROPE TOW, FRANKLIN *(previous bottom right):* ⓟ (KathDavid)

HIKING IN NH *(top left):* ⓟ (Jared_Patenaude)

SUNRISE AT PINE RIVER POND *(top right):* This is a picture of a dock with the sunlight behind it on Pine River Pond in Wakefield, NH. ⓟ (afdcapt)

SUNSET FROM LONG ISLAND BRIDGE JAN 2010 *(bottom right):* We went to reserve a campsite at Long Island Bridge. Braden and his friend went on frozen Lake Winnipesaukee and I caught this great January sunset. ⓟ (Autodoctor)

ICE GLAZED SNOW WITH BARN *(top left):* This was 4 or 5 years ago when we got a lot of freezing rain on top of the snow. The barn is on Route 136 but I'm not sure if it's in Francestown or New Boston or near the town line. Robert M. Caron (Bob_Caron)

SEVERE WEATHER 2-25-2010 - HAMPTON BEACH *(top right):* Hampton Beach's sea walls were pounded by surf due to heavy rain and strong winds.
Raychel A. Baczewski (raychel_baczewski)

DAYBREAK *(bottom left):* The morning after a wonderful snow blanket covers Gilford on the big lake! David Crook (daval2121)

DAUGHTER BRIE AT THE FLUME *(bottom right):* Recently, my daughter Brienne and I took a hike up to see the Flume in the winter. (David_Drew)

ICE FISHING MORNING *(top left):* This early morning shot was taken on Jan. 29, 2010, at sunrise. The wind was blowing snow across the lake. A pickup moved across the ice to check on a "bob house" and the sky turned pink. Taken from Center Harbor pier near the Mt. Washington. ⊕ (dbeaman)

SUNRISE AND ICE *(right):* This sunrise was very colorful. The ice added a shine to every ray of sunlight. Even though it was a very cold morning, I still took plenty of photos. ⊕ (3dogs801)

THE PUNKTS HOME *(bottom left):* We wish everyone a "Merry Christmas" and a "Happy New Year!" Each year we add a little something to our home on Blossom Street in Nashua, NH as we know the joy it brings to the little ones, teenagers and adults! The Pukts. ⊕ (The_Pukts)

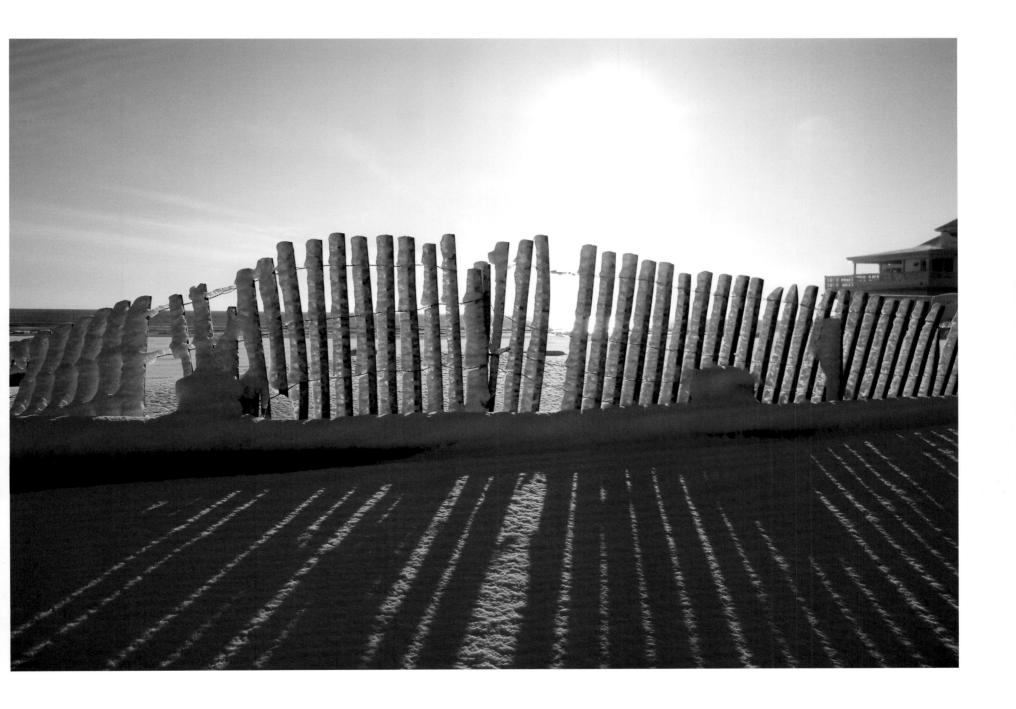

FROZEN FENCE Taken early morning at Hampton Beach just after a major ice storm and snow storm this past winter. Charles Park (charliepark)

PATS PEAK AT NIGHT *(top):* (Trier)

WINTER FUN *(bottom left):* Bill Neely out on a beautiful day snowshoeing while pulling his daughter Lily in a sled. The photo was taken along the tracks behind Epsom Central School. Brian M. McCormack (BMac)

WE MADE IT *(bottom right):* Into the water to freeze, but all for fun and a good cause: The Penguin Plunge 2010.

Kristine Freeman (umesix)

SNOW SWIRL *(top left):* My daughter Kristina Fuccillo is traveling with the ball. I love how the snow is swirling around the ball. She played in the Londonderry Youth Soccer Assoc. and the field was on West Street in Londonderry. Photo was taken in 2004 when she was 10 years old. She just turned 16. (David_Fuccillo)

FALLING IN LOVE ON THE SLOPES *(top middle):* I knew I would marry Jeff the first time he took me skiing. Now we celebrated his 40th birthday on the slopes at Pats Peak. (DanielleMartin)

GRANITE GOLD MASTER MASON *(top right):* Brisk New Hampshire winter wind! Gail M. Timmins (Brewin)

EARN YOUR TURNS ON THE STEEPS *(bottom):* (walpole411)

GOT AIR *(opposite):* A Gilford racer at Gunstock who caught an edge and was OK, but had too much time to think about the landing. ℗ (BTHoag)

JOHN FINDLAY *(top right):* This picture was taken on January 9, 2010, at a Nordic Ski race in North Conway, NH. ℗ (findlay_family)

ICE KAYAKING *(bottom right):* When you don't have snow, you can still use the frozen lakes. This is my daughter practicing ice kayaking on Lake Sunapee, NH, in Newbury Harbor. It is quite a workout. I will be making some design changes in the future for steering and paddling.
℗ (GlennPeters)

13

TAKE THE LONG WAY HOME *(opposite top left):* (Trier)

MY FAVORITE TRAM *(opposite top right):* Jennifer Dougan
(JADougan)

MY BACKYARD IN MIDDLETON *(opposite bottom):* This was taken looking out my back door after the 2008 ice storm. It almost looks like the barn door is lit up. The sun, ice and snow make such a great picture. But it sure does a number on my poor trees. Some of them had branches snapped off; some bounced back. (gdodier)

CRAWFORD PATH *(top):* Taken on Jan. 22, 2010, this sign points the way on the Crawford Path with Mt. Washington and the Montbaln Ridge behind. (manbearpig)

RACING ON THE BROADS *(top):* ℗ (mikeware)

ICE SAILING *(bottom):* This is what my family does every winter weekend on frozen Lake Sunapee, New London, NH. We put on our downhill skis and grab a kite or a kitewing and go sailing all over the lake. We were featured on NH Chronicle last Feb. 2009 and then again on Jan. 22, 2010. It is a wonderful way to enjoy the cold and ice! This photo was taken during the winter of 2009 on big Lake Sunapee. ℗ Kimberly Smith-Tuthill (sunapeeskibum)

DIXVILLE PEAK NH 1-22-10 *(top left):* ⓟ (richm)

CHERYL'S MOM *(top right):* ⓟ (coco_13baby)

LOGAN'S FACE PLANT *(bottom):* ⓟ (capers66)

FLASHBACK

MEREDITH BAY *(top):* ⓟ Susan Greenlaw (Sue Greenlaw)

ALL RIGHT ROLAND! *(bottom left):* Dad on Lake Winnisquam. ⓟ (RoxburyRoadSugarShack)

MARLEY'S BASS *(bottom right):* This is a picture of my grandson, Marley Dean, and his bass that he caught ice fishing in Henniker, our hometown! I am 62 years old and I didn't realize, after all these years, that you have to squeal and do a little dance after catching a big fish! I helped because I caught its twin later in the day! It's important to get these kids out ice fishing — littlest kid, biggest fish! ⓟ (DeanTirrell)

ICE CLIMBERS *(left):* Ice climbing in the Flume Gorge, White Mountains.
Gerry Dwyer (Thorntonfolk)

MOUNT FIELD-2/14/09 *(top right):* My husband, Kevin, and I are working on hiking all of New Hampshire's 4,000-footers. Many of our photos are of mountains located in New Hampshire's White Mountains!!! We're so lucky to have this in our backyard! Laura Morse (laura01)

RED HILL AMIGOS *(bottom right):* The Red Hill Amigos are students from Moultonborough Academy on a photo field trip to shoot motion. (BTHoag)

AIRBORNE *(opposite left top):* A perfect day where grandmother and grandson were sledding down our front hill in Nashua. Suddenly, a bump was hit and they were airborne with snow flying. A fun ride. (bjoransen)

SLEDDING FUN WITH GROWNUP KIDS *(opposite right top):* My son's fiancee from North Carolina had never enjoyed snow before. Can you imagine growing up and not ever sledding or skating or skiing? Never making a snowman or a snow fort? She was afraid to get on the sled by herself, so he hopped on with her. Cheryl Mousseau (mousseauc)

REMOTE CONTROL BALLOONS *(opposite bottom):* This was a remote control balloon festival held in Candia, NH, on the first weekend of February 2010. The balloons are 25 feet tall and operate by remote control hot air burners. The balloons came from as far away as Gatineau, Quebec. Most of the balloons are family operations where the youngsters are the pilots and the parents are the crew. The weather cooperated and allowed the balloons to fly. Sue Cassidy (pypnhot)

CANNON MOUNTAIN 1-22-10 *(above):* Cannon was incredible on January 22, 2010! Sunshine, mild temps, packed powder and powder, no wind and nearly 100 percent open. Cannon has picked up over 4 feet of snow in January and over 8 feet for the season. (Cannonman)

MT. WASH MUSH *(right):* My daughter is a musher for Muddy Paws Dog Kennel out of Jefferson and here is a photo of her with clients at the Mt. Washington Hotel on Sunday, Jan. 18, 2010. We need more snow! (robnsue2)

NHMS SNOW BOWL *(bottom left):* Jim Venne (VencowWings)

FUN IN A NH WINTER *(bottom right):* This is one of the sky bridges on the Canopy Tour at Bretton Woods, taken on Jan. 10, 2010. Isn't it gorgeous! (smylmkr)

SKIJORING IN NEW LONDON *(top left):* Skijoring New London, NH.
Elizabeth A. Marcello (lilybet)

THE FACE OF WINTER *(top middle):* I took this picture of my beloved as he was busy operating the snowblower in our driveway in Bedford, New Hampshire. He not only clears our driveway, but also a path around the house, and then clears a large section of lawn in the back for our schnauzer, Rudy, to be able to take trips outside without disappearing in the drifts. Dennis often comes in covered with snow. In this photo, he resembles Nanook of the North.
Eileen Ferguson (ehferguson)

GRANDKIDS SLEDDING *(top right):*
Eric Faller (papaeric2001)

HIGH FLYING!!! *(left):* This is a picture of Mike doing jumps on his tube in Pembroke, NH. Kevin F. Sullivan (usmcsaltydog)

STEAM IN THE SNOW 2010 *(opposite top):* I took this photo at the "Steam in the Snow" event the Conway Scenic Railroad holds every year at the beginning of January. They bring out the only operational steam locomotive ex-Canadian National 0-6-0 shunter #7470, and they run a photoshoot train for people to film and take pictures of. This year, it was on Jan. 3, 2010. We were chasing the train up north, and I set up my camera on a bridge to film it. When it started back south, I shot this. Really nice! Taken in Notchland, NH. (Trainzrule5)

SUNSET ON THE PRESIDENTIALS *(opposite bottom left):* (mikeware)

SNOWFLAKES FROM THIS MORNING *(opposite bottom right):* I took this photograph this morning of the little bit of snow we got on the ground.
Shirley Pickering (SPickering)

SUNSET ON THE HILL *(top):* Sunset on the Hill, Auburn, NH. (terryhelen)

ICE CHERRY *(opposite top left):* Windham, NH, in the morning. I just woke up and saw outside there was a lot of snow, and it was below freezing, so I went for a three-hour walk and took some photographs. Ⓟ Jessica LeBlanc (BeautyUnseen18)

BLACK AND WHITE KIND OF DAY *(opposite top right):* This photo was taken in Freedom, NH. You would think it was a black and white photo except for the brown leaf in the foreground. Ⓟ (eclair)

FALLS BY 101 *(opposite left bottom):* Falls off Route 101 in Wilton, NH. Ⓟ (mghslowell)

SUNRISE AT THE TOWN CHURCH - SOUTH HAMPTON, NH *(opposite right bottom):* I started my day walking my neighbor's black Lab through her backyard in South Hampton. We have had the most beautiful winter sunrises in 2010. I had been lucky enough to capture this moment on film. Ⓟ Gia Santosuosso (Snowfl1)

FLUME- COVERED BRIDGE IN WINTER *(top):* The picture of the bridge at the Flume nearly "did me in"! Ⓟ (sailor559)

COLD STREAM *(bottom):* Ⓟ (fjlovely)

WINTER FISHING *(top):* Saw this well-fed guy doing some fishing in Mill Brook, near Thornton. Gone in a flash when he heard the shutter click! Ⓟ Gerry Dwyer (Thorntonfolk)

WINTER IN NH *(bottom):* Ⓟ Deb McGrath (Felixx)

BOW BOBCAT *(opposite top left):* We watched this guy from our Bow home for nearly an hour while he was hunting gray squirrels. He missed and went off hungry. Ⓟ Donald Lowe (dondi6)

YOUNG BULL *(opposite top right):* Young bull moose licking salt in road. Holding up traffic. Ⓟ (mooseman54)

WHY DO TURKEYS CROSS THE ROAD? *(opposite bottom):* Ⓟ Dorie McKeeman (dmck3)

CHLOE *(top):*  (marilyn3)

ALL THAT'S LEFT OF OUR SNOWMAN ON FEBRUARY 26 - TRY EXPLAINING THAT ONE TO A 3-YEAR-OLD!! *(bottom right):* This snowman was built in Charlestown, NH, on our deck the morning of 2/24 after we received all the snow. Our 4-year-old daughter loved him and would check on him during the day to make sure he was still there. That was until after a night of rain, when she looked on the deck, and this is what she found. She ran to her dad, shouting, "Daddy! Daddy! My snowman is gone. He melted...and he left his hat!" (MicheleWestney)

WHAT SNOW! *(bottom left):* Newfoundlands just love winter in Dunbarton, NH. (jkeefe)

5-YEAR-OLD LUCAS' 1ST GAME *(previous top left):* Raymond Bisson (RayBisson)

MILL BROOK WATERFALL *(previous top middle):* At the waterfall on Mill Brook near Thornton. Lot of energy going over those rocks! Thankfully we have not had any flooding this far north, but I pity those in the flood regions of the state. Gerry Dwyer (Thorntonfolk)

PEACEFUL STREAM *(previous top right)* This picture shows the true tranquility of the New Hampshire outdoors. (mcharbonneau)

ROBIN EGGS *(previous middle left):* A robin made a nest in a rhododendron in my parents' front yard. It's close enough to the ground that I was able to take pictures.
Meghan Poznanski Hardy (map1120)

BLEEDING HEART BLOOMIN' *(previous middle right):* A nice surprise in spite of the cold temps and snow flurries! Carol Nicholeris (MtnLuvah)

SWIFTWATER RESCUE TRAINING *(previous bottom left):* Participants in a Lifesaving Resources' Swiftwater Rescue training course practice advancing a rescue boat into the face of a low head dam to rescue a victim caught in the river's hydraulic. The course is open to fire, rescue, EMS and law enforcement personnel and is designed to provide them with the skills and knowledge required to safely and effectively respond to incidents in, on and around both static and moving water environments. (lifesaving)

FAMILY OUTING *(previous bottom middle):* Taken on pond in Merrimack, NH.
Wayne Stribling (wstrib)

CORNISH/WINDSOR BRIDGE - CORNISH *(previous bottom right):* Working my way on photographing all the covered bridges in NH. I have 28 so far out of 57. (canterburyshoe)

POWDER PUFF *(top left):* Taken near pond in Merrimack, NH. Wayne Stribling (wstrib)

DOUBLE RAINBOW *(top right):* (MartinsNH)

STRATHAM, NH *(bottom right):* My neighbor's barn taken during a beautiful sunrise.
(brockily61)

SPRINGTIME AT THE BELKNAP MILL *(top left):* A few shots from downtown Laconia on a beautiful spring on 4/26/10. Chuck Healey (ChuckHealey)

DAFFODILS *(top right):* Put the flag out for spring. (marshamlanier)

GARDEN WALKWAY *(bottom left):* While out for a walk one day, I saw this beautiful walkway in a neighbor's yard. Lydia Williams (fouz_ball)

THIN ICE! *(bottom right):* Early ice melting at Meredith Bay, Meredith, NH. March 31, 2006. Benjamin L. Nelson (Benji)

COLORS OF A DYING SUN *(top left):* Just driving home from the Great North Woods and caught this sunset going down over a ridge. (enchantedearthgallery)

PORTSMOUTH NORTH CHURCH TULIPS *(right):* Photo of Portsmouth taken early morning during the month of May. The North Church is the iconic Portsmouth landmark, framed by a lovely array of Tulips with a striking blue sky. (NHLOON)

FIRE IN THE SKY! *(bottom left):* I took this a couple of years ago of Little Great Bay, in Newington, NH. J.J. Fallon (JFallon)

VIEW FOR TWO Taken at grandmother's house last spring on Mother's Day. View is of Great Bay in Durham, NH. Ⓤ Ashley Herrin (ashlynne.herrin)

SPRING ON THE FARM *(opposite left):* While photographing covered bridges, I came across this farm in Newport and it just caught my eye and I snapped a couple pictures. (canterburyshoe)

FOG ON ALTON BAY, APRIL 1, 2010 *(top right):* Mark E. Foster (Mark_Foster)

SWOLLEN FALLS - MARLBOROUGH, NH *(bottom right):* Kyle Rider (sportingimage11)

MT. LINCOLN *(opposite top left):* Shot from the Franconia Ridge trail from the summit of Mt. Lafayette. (enchantedearthgallery)

SPRING TIME AT THE STATE HOUSE *(opposite top right):* (Blue_Ultra)

VIEW FROM MT. MAJOR *(opposite bottom):* Panoramic photo from the top of Mt. Major in Alton, overlooking Lake Winnipesaukee. Daniel Skafas (dskafas)

CRAWFORD NOTCH *(left):* This was taken on an early morning "moose run" looking for wildlife. Crawford Notch has some absolutely breathtaking scenery. (dakema)

A REFLECTION OF THE MONADNOCK REGION *(top right):* Kyle Rider (sportingimage11)

MOUNT WASHINGTON FROM NEAR THE SUMMIT OF MOUNT JEFFERSON *(bottom right):* (japerk57)

MIST ON WATER - EXETER, NH *(opposite top left):* 🄌 (cdodge)

TALL FALLS *(opposite right):* He's 5-foot-3. 🄌 (RochesterRockhound)

ZIP LINE, BRETTON WOODS SKI AREA *(opposite bottom left):* Bretton woods, NH zip line! What an awesome experience! 🄌 Kristie Drapeau and Dan Perry (dankristie)

CONNOR WOULDN'T STOP REELING BECAUSE HE WAS SO EXCITED *(top left):* 🄌 Jason and Angela Blake (blakesters)

ON TOP OF THE WORLD *(top right):* 🄌 (krystil23)

MAIDEN VOYAGE *(bottom):* 🄌 (matrum56)

43

HEADING FOR THE WATER *(opposite top left):* Cole and Saylor taking an early swim at Dewey Beach in Sunapee. The day was really warm, but the water was still freezing, considering it was May! (myrefair)

FISHING *(opposite right):* (ManderlynRose)

MARTY COOLING OFF *(opposite middle left):* (MudgieGirls)

LOOKING FORWARD TO NH SUMMER *(opposite bottom left):* Rhiannon Ferman (megnut21)

BUILDING A SAND CASTLE *(above):* (garota007)

LULU AND I *(opposite):* My friend and I went hiking with our dogs. This is Lulu, my 5-year-old golden retriever, and myself on top of Mt. Pemigewasset. (jessicaallison05)

CLEAN FUN *(top left):* This is such a dirty sport locally every month, where getting dirty is such clean fun!
Mike Kirwan (thekirwanartdept)

AMPHIBIOUS CAR 4-3-2010 *(top right):* Easter Sunday on Lake Winnisquam. Michele Collins (chupto)

BREAKING GROUND *(bottom):* Oxen help expand the international community garden at Brookside Congregational Church in Manchester.
Dawn Brockett (DBrockett)

STATIC SLIDE *(top):* (StaceyE.Kegelman)

SNOW IN MAY *(bottom left):* I took this photo of my three sons on the morning of May 1, 1987 in Manchester, NH. A cold rain on April 30th changed over to a heavy, wet snow that knocked down some very old, large trees. And yes, that IS forsythia already blooming in the background!
Brenda Gikas (bgikas)

SPRINKLER FUN *(bottom right):* Granddaughter's first experience with the sprinkler. (kare115)

FLASHBACK

GETTING WET *(top left):* Alison C. Woods Baker (awoodsbaker)

SPRING MUD *(top middle):* (jwaynejane)

PLAY BALL *(top right):* Baseball and springtime go hand in hand and is truly a NH family-friendly sport! Deb McGrath (Felixx)

PUPPY HUGS *(bottom):* Katherine Donovan (Artgeek21)

SISTERLY LOVE *(top left):*
(mpothier)

KISSES - APRIL 2010 *(top right):*
Jennifer Lopez (Momto3Divas)

READY TO RIDE *(bottom left)*
(MRJSMom)

ALL SMILES *(bottom right):*
(leessa64)

TT IN THE TULIPS   Maeve of Londonderry, NH, enjoys Auntie's tulip garden. (AuntieMary1)

SPRING FLOWERS *(top left):*
Cedric Carrier (roadracer318)

WALKWAY BEAUTY *(right):* This is on Front Street in Exeter. Kristine Freeman (umesix)

STATE FLOWER *(bottom left):*
(SUSANLAVOIE)

MAKE A WISH *(left):* I was frolicking through the fields one day trying to find something to take a picture of and I decided to try and see if I could take a picture of the last seed on a dandelion flying away. I sat there for about 10 minutes until I finally got the perfect shot. ☺ Devin Donohue (jaxo)

FLOWERS *(top right):* My backyard in Rochester, NH, trying out my new camera. ☺ (larry3)

TULIPS IN THE WIND *(bottom right):* ☺ (karenrrw)

PANSIES!!! *(opposite):* Flowers feed my soul! Robin M. St. Pierre (bumblemom)

BEE *(left):* This was taken in Nashua, NH. Kristi Durkin (kristi_durkin)

CAUGHT IN THE ACT *(top right):* Chipmunk raiding the feeder outside my window looking for peanuts. (snowshoe)

SWAN *(bottom right):* The Swans of Eel Pond, Rye, NH. Deb McGrath (Felixx)

OWL HOUSE TENANTS *(top left):* These are two baby squirrels that were raised in an owl house intended for saw whet owls.
Jim Andrews (Deadhead)

BLUEBIRD BALLET *(top right):* The victorious male bluebird is checking his wings after a battle in the snow with another male. June Harris (madgardener)

BABY ROBINS *(bottom left):* Peter Gray (PeterGray)

RED CARDINAL DAD FEEDING ITS BABY *(bottom right):* One day we discovered a bird's nest in a small pine tree outside my bedroom window. When we went inside to see the view, it turned out that we had the perfect view and started to watch the mother nesting every day and then watched the eggs hatch to watch them grow to the day they left the nest. (kimberrr)

OFF TO GATHER NESTING MATERIALS
(top left): Photo taken in Bedford, NH.
Eileen Ferguson (ehferguson)

**COPPAL HOUSE FARM - GETTING READY
FOR THE CORN MAZE** *(top right):*
(nmbrzgal)

A MORNING CANTER *(bottom):* As the
warming sun in late May burns off the
morning fog along the New Hampshire
Seacoast, this beautiful horse enjoys a slow
canter across his pasture, which at the
time was blazing with these bright yellow
dandelions. Frank Silva (Fsilva)

FOUR GOLDENS *(opposite):* This is what happens at our house when we are outside and the dogs aren't. ℗ Mark S. LeBlanc, Sr. (marksleblanc)

JAKKIE'S FIRST BOAT RIDE OF 2010 *(left):* The first boat ride Jakkie took with her orange life vest on Berry Pond in Moultonborough, April 26. ℗ (alively5)

ZIPPY ON SAFARI *(top right):* Exploring spring sprouts. ℗ Suzan Grondin (73077)

NICK & THE TURTLE *(bottom right):* ℗ (suz_steele)

BEAR CUB (top): Bear cub seen here in our backyard in Bethlehem, NH.
Ⓟ Diane Anderson (Kiana)

FURRY GUESTS - MOMMA WITH PUPS (bottom left): A family of foxes decided to take up residence next to our home in Lee. This is but one of many pictures taken since their arrival. Ⓟ (SCSmitty)

BABY PORCUPINE (bottom right):
Ⓟ (suz_steele)

WET TURKEY A turkey crosses the road in Portsmouth, NH, near the Great Bay Wildlife Refuge. Ⓟ (jonathanmayhew)

BLUE HERON *(top):* ⓟ Peter Gray (PeterGray)

ROBIN *(bottom left):* This was taken in Nashua, NH. ⓟ Kristi Durkin (kristi_durkin)

LOON *(bottom right):* Loon at Willard Pond in Antrim. ⓟ Jennifer Szuch (jszuch)

SUMMER

KIDS LOVE KAYAKING *(previous top left)*: Family kayaking on the Saco River in North Conway, Conway Lake and Umbagog Lake in NH is the best! (dotdash12)

BAER ROAD MORNING *(previous top middle)*: Morning mist on Baer Road. (dawne19)

CANNEY HILL GILMANTON IRON WORKS *(previous top right)*: A relaxing spot for family and friends.....my backyard. (kkgilmanton)

NA-NA-NA-NA-NA-NA *(previous middle left)*: This Canadian goose was really giving what-for to the other geese. Eileen Ferguson (ehferguson)

BEAR RESIDENTS MEET SOPHIE C *(previous middle right)*: The Sophie C is the oldest operating floating post office in the U.S. She provides mail service to islands on Lake Winnipesaukee and takes lake visitors for a guided tour each day beginning in June and ending in September. These daily mail deliveries date back to 1892. This photo was taken while the Sophie C made a mail stop at the 780-acre Bear Island's one-room post office. Island residents gather on the dock each day to greet the mail boat. Lydia Williams (fouz_ball)

SILHOUETTE ON LAUREL LAKE *(previous bottom left)*: This photo was taken at dusk on the Fourth of July on Laurel Lake. (leorajanelle)

DO YOU SEE WHAT I SEE? *(previous bottom middle)*: They all walked to the fence to see the dog on the other side. Just seeing them all at the same time doing the same thing was priceless. Kristine Freeman (umesix)

HAYING THE OLD-FASHIONED WAY *(previous bottom right)*: Duane Cross (duaneups)

COLORS OF RYE *(top)*: Early morning sunrises at Rye are often breathtaking. This, along with the warm, fresh salty breezes, makes for an enjoyable experience that should be tried by all. Jack W. Parker (jackwparker)

CAMERON VACATIONING AT RYE, NH *(bottom)*: Cameron Cuttita comes down with her parents from Vermont each year to boogie board at the great NH beaches. Her grandparents Bill and Maureen Binning, enjoy their grandkids, and all 10 of them stay for two weeks each year on the Seacoast. Mike Egad (megansnh)

8-8-2010 6:13 *(top left):* A morning of balloon chasing. 🄟 (Molly_Kaiser)

CAMPTON VILLAGE *(bottom left):* 🄟 Frank and Barb LaJeunesse (franknbabs)

SUN COMING UP OVER SUNCOOK RIVER *(top right):* I was able to catch the beautiful colors in the sky as the sun was coming up. The air was so cold that the steam added a special touch! 🄟 Michele Natali (natali790)

CINNAMON RAINBOWS SURF SHOP *(bottom right):* Hampton, NH.
🄟 Taylor Marie Trainor (ttaybaybay)

DOUBLE RAINBOWS *(top left):* A summer 2010 view that I caught after a couple nice summer rains. Taken in our backyard in Groveton, NH. Rainbows over Cape Horn and Mt. Hutchins. Ⓤ Elaine Richards Gray (emma54)

SUNRISE OVER MEREDITH BAY 08-18-10 *(right):* Ⓤ Becky F. Moss (NHone)

BARN, DOGS, SUNFLOWER *(bottom left):* Ⓤ Mark S. LeBlanc, Sr. (marksleblanc)

PORTSMOUTH TUGBOATS Becky F. Moss (NHone)

HILLS POND SUNSET *(opposite left):* This photo is from our home on Hills Pond in Alton Bay. ℗ Tim Courounis (pcandtc)

SUNSET ON NEWFOUND LAKE *(top right):* Spent the week on Newfound Lake with the whole family for the first time in many years. What could be a better way to end a day of swimming and sailing with my children and grandchildren than to take in this beautiful sunset?
℗ Lauris Simon (lesimonsez)

SEAGULL ON GRAFTON POND *(bottom right):*
℗ Jennifer Dougan (JADougan)

HEAD OVER HEELS FOR SOFTBALL *(top left):* We are the Diamond Gems and we are "Head over Heels" for softball! Our team represented New Hampshire at the Nationals this summer.
Ⓟ Mary Pelrine (Pelrineboys)

CHELSEA DEMERS WINNING FORM AT WOMEN'S STATE AM *(right):* Chelsea Demers on the 16th tee drives her ball into the fairway at the 2010 NHGWA State Amateur Championship held at Cocheco CC in Dover, NH. Ⓟ Mike Egad (megansnh)

FOOTBALL FUN *(bottom left):* The Merrimack Tomahawks seniors have a little pre-season fun! Don't be surprised by their cheerfulness...they are ready for Friday Night Football! Ⓟ Mary Pelrine (Pelrineboys)

ONE MORE OFF THE BUCKET LIST *(top left):* 14,000 feet — what a view! (alton06)

ZIP LINE TRAINING *(top right):* Officer Dana Dexter at the ropes course at Camp Spaulding in Concord. Members of the Concord Police Department participated in the ropes course on a recent training day. The zip line was one of the favorite activities. (woodslipmukhouk)

A DAY IN THE LIFE *(bottom):* Summer time fun includes many of my favorite people, places, and outdoor activities. And luckily, because I live in NH, as do three of my five grandchildren, I am able to combine all three! Deb McGrath (Felixx)

NEVER FORGET THE SUMMER OF 2010 Young men enjoying the surf in Rye, NH. Mike Egad (megansnh)

JERICHO STATE PARK 4-WHEELING *(top left):* A family trip to Berlin and Jericho State Park for some recreational OHRVing. (woodslipmukhouk)

BALLOONS OVER MILFORD AND AMHERST *(top middle):* Early one morning in August, balloons went over my house in Milford, so I followed them until they landed in Amherst. (rizzochris)

SWAINS LAKE *(top right):* Summer vacation at Swains Lake. Glenn Fournier (phroggie)

HIKING PRESIDENTIAL RANGE *(bottom):* Hiking has become a favorite of Mike's, recent graduate of Prospect Mtn. High School - thanks to the Outing Club and science teacher Joe Derrick. (hockeymom23)

COOL CARS *(top):* More than 100 cars attended the 11th annual "Cruisin' At The Hop" car show in Bath, NH. Sponsored by At The Hop Ice Cream Shop and the Connecticut River Valley Cruisers. More than $1,250 was raised through raffle prizes and a 50/50 drawing. All proceeds went to the Bath Fire Association and the Pine Grove Grange. Nancy Lusby (nelusby)

KAYAKING 7 A.M., RYE, NH *(bottom left):* Early kayakers off Jenness Beach, Rye, NH. Mike Egad (megansnh)

WAITING *(bottom right):* The day has begun, the row boats are all in a row, and everyone is sleeping in...except for me. Mary Pelrine (Pelrineboys)

NICE CATCH *(opposite top left):* The mountains, the coast, and the lakes of NH are phenomenal, especially when spent with those I love. And it is an added bonus when I capture one of these priceless moments with my camera! Deb McGrath (Felixx)

NEWFOUND LAKE GIRL *(opposite top right):* My mother as a young girl would go up to Newfound Lake for the summer staying with her aunt and uncle. This is where she learned to love swimming. (ne8w)

COOLING OFF *(opposite bottom):* This little one was enjoying the fountain at the park in North Conway, NH, on an extremely hot day. Kristine Freeman (umesix)

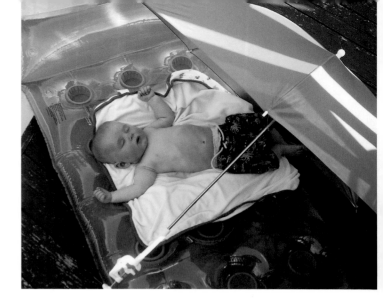

SUNSET RUN *(left):* North Hampton beach sunset. Looking for sea glass and running a few sprints is always a lovely evening activitiy. Amy Dube (AmyDube)

GARRETT LOUNGING BY THE POOL *(top right):* Mike Hayward, Jr. (mikejr)

THE GREAT PYRAMID AT HAMPTON BEACH 2010 *(bottom right):* I had all my nieces and nephews down from Canada and I took them to Hampton Beach. (evets2011)

SAND ART AT HAMPTON (Bics_pics)

ON THE BOAT *(top left):* Another priceless summer time moment captured with my camera! ⓤ Deb McGrath (Felixx)

FIRST OLYMPIAN POSE *(top right):*
ⓤ Steven W. Andersen (StevenWAndersen)

SLAY THE BEAST!!! *(bottom left):* My daughter Laura and her boyfriend Ryan slaying the T rex (tree).
ⓤ Kathleen Brodeur (Brodeurhouse)

FUN WITH BUBBLES *(bottom right):* ⓤ (mikeware)

COLE IN BUCKET *(left):* Newbury, NH Ⓤ Jessica Bates Chandler (twinboys08)

LONDON WATCHING HIS FIRST RACE *(right top):* Ⓤ Kristie Drapeau and Dan Perry (dankristie)

SPLASH BOMB *(right bottom):* Ⓤ (roger999)

FLINGING PIZZA DOUGH *(right):* New Ipswich, NH. Taking a chance flinging the dough. Liz Walton (lizwalton)

MUD VOLLEYBALL *(left):* This photo was taken at the Mud Volleyball game during annual Labor Day festivities in Francestown. The Village Improvement Society has been a sponsor since 1911, but has only sponsored mud volleyball for the past 10 years. The events take place over a three-day period to raise money for unfunded town projects. I think those who as children loved to get down and dirty making mud pies especially love this event! Deb McGrath (Felixx)

NANNY'S RIDE *(opposite left):* Strafford, NH. Melissa Libby (ashmiss034)

SMALL TOWN FOURTH OF JULY PARADE *(opposite top right):*
Paulette Lemoine (lemoinepn)

ACCIDENTAL CATCH *(opposite middle right):* We were fishing off of the Isles of Shoals and this was on the end of the line. Fortunately for the lobster, it was returned to the sea. It weighed in at 20 pounds.
Harry Burton (swimdog)

SUCCESS AT THE END OF A SCARY DRIVE *(opposite bottom right):* I never realized why people were so proud to post the "This car climbed Mt. Washington" bumper sticker until I made the drive myself. What an experience! A little terrifying at times, but adrenaline-pumping too. I earned that bumper sticker! (NinaFouch)

TAKING THE PLUNGE! *(top left):* Sarah Patsos (UNH '07) & Kevin Regan (UNH '08) met and fell in love while at college. She was from Connecticut, and he was from South Boston but they both agreed there was no place they'd rather have their wedding than in NH. They were married on July 31, 2010, in Sunapee and topped off the weekend celebrations with "the plunge" off Sarah's family's dock on Lake Sunapee in Newbury. (scribbles231)

TOUCH DOWN *(right):* Just as we were getting ready to leave, I got to see a balloon touch the water. Thanks to my sister Jeanette for pushing me to share this shot! Michele Natali (natali790)

RIDING THE RAPIDS IN STYLE *(bottom left):* Michael Pollini (mikepollini)

SUNRISE ON THE ANDROSCOGGIN RIVER   My husband and I got up early to kayak before sunrise. There were moose, loon and osprey all around. What a beautiful day we had!   Ann Leahy (hebgbs00)

MEMORIAL BRIDGE *(top):* Ⓟ Raymond Bisson (RayBisson)

NH COUNTRY BARN *(bottom):* Ⓟ (jemmfarm)

AMAZING SUNSET *(opposite left):* This amazing sunset was shot at Lake Massabesic after a storm on July 10, 2010. Ⓟ Linda Bacon (lindalu5)

GARDEN OF FAMILY AND FRIENDS *(opposite top right):* This is in the Justice of the Peace, Garden of Family & Friends. Ⓟ Linda Mulligan (Linda)

GOOD MORNING EAST INLET *(opposite bottom right):* Ⓟ Jennifer Dougan (JADougan)

AFTER THE RAIN AT LAKE KANASATKA, MOULTONBOROUGH, NH - AUGUST 2008 *(top left):* ℗ (rcaube)

SUNSET OVER UMBAGOG LAKE *(top right):* Camping with friends at Umbagog State Park last weekend and caught this beautiful sunset. I was also on the beach with other friends to view the sunrise that very morning. ℗ (The_Incredible_P)

WENTWORTH BOAT BASIN *(bottom):* ℗ Rosemary Carter-Molnar (rocee5)

BABY GULLS *(top):* Baby seagulls at the Isles of Shoals. ℗ Skip Averell (35REM)

LOON FLUTTERING HIS WINGS *(bottom):* Clough Pond, in Loudon, NH. ℗ Jo-Ann Matthews (JoAnnM)

MARCHING IN WOLFEBORO'S JULY 4TH PARADE *(top left):* This is the only way to march in a parade — me and my rubber ducky! Mary Pelrine (Pelrineboys)

MOLLY BRUSHING HER TEETH *(top right):* I decided to see if I could get a photo of my cat Molly with a toothbrush (I work for a dental benefits company). This one was the cutest. She does look like she is brushing. Debbie LaValley (dlv1)

ENJOYING LIFE AT THE LAKE *(bottom):* We take our two golden retrievers to Silver Lake in Harrisville each summer and they love floating on the raft. They borrowed the goggles from the grandkids. Jacob MacKay (hillsidefarmnh)

KOBY *(top left):* Practicing for Dock Dogs. (Jenna95)

DOG *(top right):* (PatCullityBezanson)

LOBSTERS AT A COOKOUT *(bottom left):* The highlight at cookouts and parties is when the lobsters are served!
Dorothy A Lewis (DAL)

WHALE WATCH *(bottom right):* Our first whale watch with Granite State Whale Watch in Rye, NH, during our June vacation. (2boxers)

SUSAN'S HORSES *(opposite):* Mark S. LeBlanc, Sr. (marksleblanc)

THE WABBIT'S IN THE GARDEN AGAIN *(top left):* Peter Gray (PeterGray)

COWLICK *(right):* (mrgames2)

WILLY AND BAILY THE POTBELLY PIG *(bottom left):* Willy, the son of a friend, is feeding Baily an apple. Baily lives at a residence in New Ipswich, NH. Kathleen Ashe (1313pig)

DINNER TIME! *(top left):* Look who came to dinner. ⓟ (Kiana)

BALD EAGLE *(right):* Banded bald eagle, a resident of Bow Lake in Northwood, NH. This female is one of two banded eagles nesting on Bow Lake. The two eagles were both banded in Maine and are the first banded pair from that state known to be nesting. ⓟ (NHLOON)

MOOSE DETOUR *(bottom left):* We were on a motorcycle ride through the White Mountains and came across this female moose on the side of the road. ⓟ Marie Pullin (Mpullin)

ESKIMO KISSES Duane Cross (duaneups)

DRAGONFLY *(top left):* Kelley Downs (bluemoose67)

AMARYLLIS DISPLAY *(top right):* I winter my amaryllis bulbs in containers and drag them out to the garage in April and always get stunning results. (corykm1031)

I GOT SOMETHING ON MY NOSE! *(bottom):* (loudonphoto)

TILTON PARK *(previous top left):* Cole taking fall pictures at Tilton park with wagon.
(colesmommynicole)

TUCKER BROOK FALLS *(previous top middle):* Of all the waterfalls we are blessed with here in New Hampshire, this has to be, in my opinion, the nicest! It is located in Tucker Brook Town Forest in Milford, NH. (djazz33)

SITTING WITH THE PUMPKINS *(previous top right):* Jaime Morin (Jaimerrn)

FOLLOW ME *(previous middle left):* Grandson playing youth football for Plymouth Huskies vs. Milford and teammates. Picture taken on on Sept. 19, 2010.
Bruce Covert (BRUCEANDKAREN)

BACK YARD INTO THE WOODS *(previous middle right):* In my back yard last year on September 17th...wonder if it will look the same this Friday. (deborah514)

MOOSE *(previous left bottom):* Saw the moose beside the road just before entering the 13-mile woods in Errol, NH. (scaplette)

FALL BRIDGE *(previous bottom middle):* (Trier)

COMMON MERGANSER *(previous bottom right):* (katespics)

PUMPKIN WAGON *(top left):* (ADanahy)

BRIDGE *(top right):* George "Skip" Mauzy (islandskip)

FALL FOLIAGE *(bottom right):* This photo was taken at Ossipee Lake, NH.
(bupster2010)

FALL SUNRISE IN DUBLIN, NH *(top left):* We took a ride to Pack Monadnock & Silver Lake in Harrisville, NH. Jo-Ann Matthews (JoAnnM)

FALL COLORS *(top right):* This lonely leaf was in the pond above Maple Falls in Candia. (Diana)

OCTOBER MORNING MEREDITH, NH *(bottom left):* Early morning mist over Lake Winnipesaukee. (TheMount)

NUTS *(bottom right):* Squirrels will eat well this fall. (RobertFemenella)

AUTUMN SUNRISE OVER MASCOMA LAKE *(top left):* Tom Brodeur (Mapeco)

TREES *(right):* Hiking in the the National Forest. (snapshot101)

MOONRISE *(bottom left):* Rene M. Thibault (renethibault)

FOLIAGE ⓘ (NewHampshirerocks)

RIGHT TIME OF DAY *(opposite left):* I arrived at this Concord New Hampshire cemetery just in the nick of time to catch a few setting sun foliage shots. Ⓟ Cory Morrill (corykm1031)

SWIFT RIVER FOLIAGE *(top right):* Taken along the Kancamaugus Highway. The Swift River with beautiful foliage framing it. Ⓟ Jon Winslow (NHLOON)

TREES *(bottom right):* Ⓟ George "Skip" Mauzy (islandskip)

MASSABESIC SUNRISE *(top left):* Glenn Peters (GlennPeters)

FALL SAILING *(right):* Took this shot of a Nacra 5.5 catamaran as it flew by me while I was out sailing on Lake Winnipesaukee on Columbus Day. (ChuckHealey)

PORT VS. STARBOARD TACK *(middle left):* (mikeware)

RUDY & DENNIS, PILLSBURY STATE PARK, WASHINGTON, NH *(bottom left):* Rudy, Dennis and Eileen love camping, hiking and kayaking at Pillsbury State Park, Washington, NH. Eileen Ferguson (ehferguson)

OUZO PLUNGE GROUP *(top):* This is the Ouzo Plunge. Every year, my friends take a brisk swim at Pleasant Pond in Francestown, NH. It's a bit cold, but nothing that ouzo and some laughter can't solve. (mrbuk2001)

COACH'S TALK *(bottom left):* This is the Capital City Vipers Tiny Mite Team pre-game; coaches talk to the team.
Ian Tewksbury (itewksbury)

FLY FISHING *(bottom right):* (charlister1962)

WALKING THE WIRE! *(top left):* My grandkids Ryan and Kennah were on the high wires, wooden steps and zip slides at the Monkey Trunks in Tamworth, NH. The highest pole is way above the trees and houses in the area. Not for the faint of heart!
(oblossum)

RAPPELLING *(right):* Leslie Bingham Bennett (LeslieJBB)

SOCCER *(bottom left):* (lcroteau)

BIRD HUNTING   Bird hunting at the foot of the Sandwich Mountain Range. 🔊 (SCes00)

MUDBOWL 2010 *(opposite):* (BradHall)

WOODSMAN CONTEST *(top left):* (Spottie_and_Daisy)

HE CALLS THIS DEERFIELD FARM *(bottom left):* He says his name is John Kennedy. I met him on a road trip in Deerfield, NH, Route 43. (KeepNitRealGf)

BAYSIDE *(bottom right):* (bayside)

DEERFIELD FAIR *(top left):* Jeannie Woolf (jmw22)

I CAN READ! *(top right):* Our son is showing his Nomy and Opa that he can read, too, while relaxing on Mount Kearsage in Warner, NH. Megan A.E. Guerra (maeguerra5)

MADISON & RILEY TRYING TO BREAK A BUBBLE *(bottom):* Beach trip with four generations of families. Jo-Ann Matthews (JoAnnM)

GREAT FUN ON THE TRACTOR RIDE AT MEADOW LEDGE FARM *(top left):* This was taken at Meadow Ledge Farm in Loudon, NH. An afternoon of apples, pumpkins, homemade cider, doughnuts and lots of laughs! Mandie Rowell-Hagan (MandieRowellHagan)

SECOND AUTUMN *(bottom left):* Our 15-month-old son is enjoying helping his father rake the leaves with his own rake in Dunbarton, NH. Michelle Morin (dmhm2010)

KATIE'S LEAF HAT *(bottom right):* Katie playing in the backyard leaf pile. (MySweetKate)

FLASHBACK

MARY ALICE *(opposite top left):* This photo was taken in October of 1991 on our front lawn in Westmoreland. (maryaduke)

740-POUND PUMPKIN BEING CARVED *(opposite top right):* This photo is from the 2008 Pumpkin Festival in Keene. This shows a 740-pound pumpkin which we carved for the Festival's Giant Pumpkin Carving Contest. Our entry won first place in the contest and drew hundreds who watched us complete the five-hour carving process. The carvers were Janice Wooding and Pat Johnson. (jan050957)

LINWOOD SILLY GIRLS *(opposite bottom left):* Playing in the leaves at big brother's and big sister's soccer games. (chefdirk)

LOOK WHAT I CAUGHT! *(opposite bottom right):* (nhshutterbug)

KEENE PUMPKIN FESTIVAL *(top left):* My kids and I enjoyed the Keene Pumpkin Festival in Keene, NH. (wiggymoney)

MAKING CIDER WITH BUMPA *(right):* This is a picture of my father in-law, Kevin Borrows, and his grandson, Nathan Jones, making apple cider in Merrimack, NH, in the fall of 2006. (jpjonesy2)

HURDY GURDY MAN *(bottom left):* (Spottie_and_Daisy)

GETTING READY FOR HALLOWEEN
(opposite): Molly, age 2, pushes her huge pumpkin to the front steps. Ⓟ (MartiWarren)

PUMPKIN AMONG PUMPKINS *(top left):* My daughter's first trip to Brookdale Farm! Apples and pumpkins.
Ⓟ Erin-Anne Lemieux (MichaelLemieux)

PICKING THE PERFECT PUMPKIN *(top right):*
Ⓟ (heidiphil)

MY BEAUTIFUL GRANDAUGHTER
(bottom): J&F Farms in Derry, NH. Ⓟ (mikeatbp)

PICKING OUT HIS PUMPKIN *(top):* Our grandson Michael wanted to pick out his own pumpkin, and, of course, he picked out one that weighed more than him. 💬 (pennyk)

MASON IN THE FALL *(bottom left):* A beautiful photo of Mason taken by his grandpa after his baptism at East Church in Concord. 💬 (becs5115)

PUMPKINS *(bottom right):* 💬 (caron3)

PUMPKINS APLENTY *(opposite):* My daughter and I spent a fabulous fall afternoon at Beech Hill Farm in Hopkinton. We enjoyed ice cream on a day that was as hot as in summer. We gave our "hellos" to the animals, including pigs, donkeys, cows, goats, bunnies, chickens and peacocks. It's a shame Charlie Brown missed the Great Pumpkin because he paid a bountiful visit, leaving many pallets and a full wagon of those big orange beauties. This quick after-school trip became a beautiful memory for always. 💬 (clrice9)

MAPLE TREE *(top right):* The maple tree was taken Oct. 31, 2009 off Parade Road in Laconia. I was looking for some fall color. ℗ (billtiz)

FIELD OF GOURDS *(left):* ℗ (young)

AN AFTERNOON CREATION... *(bottom right):* Out in the yard, my daughter and I were having a picnic lunch. We began to collect leaves for fun, then placed them in patterns and shapes. Against the freshly cut lawn, this "creation" really stood out. ℗ (mhall27)

SABBADAY FALLS LOWER STEP *(opposite left):* The falls lower step. ℗ (capers66)

ELF SHELTER *(opposite top right):* Tucked beneath a road barrier, this toadstool along South Merrimack Road in Hollis measured 8 inches across—a perfect place for forest critters to stay dry. ℗ Dorie McKeeman (dmck3)

FIRST FROST *(opposite middle right):* I captured this when we were walking my son to school. ℗ Debi Rapson (DrDebi)

PINE CONE *(opposite bottom right):* ℗ (colbyy)

NATURE'S CROWN *(opposite top left):* Bill Fullam (WilliamFullam)

ENCHANTED SUNSET *(opposite top right):* Shot on Cemetery Hill in New Boston on Sept. 12, 2010, overlooking Mount Monadnock. One of my favorite peaks to shoot from. (CynthiaM.YardeKiernan)

CHOCURA BRIDGE *(opposite bottom):* This photo was taken at the wooden bridge next to Lake Chocura. A beautiful New Hampshire setting. Jon Winslow (NHLOON)

DOUBLE RAINBOW *(top):* Double rainbow in Errol, NH. (MartinsNH)

MEREDITH BAY AWAKENING *(bottom):* I pass by this spot at Meredith Bay, and this time of year, and certain days, this is what I see. The only way this could have been any better is if my boat was sitting on that dock ready for a day of fun and fishing. Paul Johnstone (paulj56)

I SEE YOU! *(left):*  (Spottie_and_Daisy)

PERFECT TRIO *(top right):* After going apple picking a few years ago, I decided to take a drive by the Silver Ranch Stables in Jaffrey; that's when I caught this beautiful moment. (melmartin)

AUTUMN REFLECTIONS *(bottom right):* Fred Martin (Weeks)

PAWS OUT *(top):* I think the photo speaks for it self. Molly doesn't need a pumpkin to look scary for Halloween. Susan B. Hoskins (Sookey)

MISSY LOVES APPLES! *(bottom left):* Was taken at Lull Farm in Hollis, NH. We went pumpkin and apple picking; it was my dog's first time. She loved all the new smells in the air and the different people coming up to greet her. (DARTANEUN)

JESSEE PICKING HER PUMPKIN *(bottom right):* Dana L. Weir (lifesmoments)

HOPE TO SEE YOU AGAIN SOON *(top left):*
Duane Cross (duaneups)

ELK IN THE FALL *(top right):* This photo was taken in Hillsboro, NH, on a farm. The backdrop was a nice setting with the colors of fall coming in! (gailmoose527)

FEEDING MOOSE *(bottom):* Bill Mckee (ridgerunner)

YOUNG BLACK BEAR *(top left):* A young black bear surveying the landscape for food. ⓟ Walt Rogers (skierharley)

COW IN FOG *(top right):* This photo was taken in Rollinsford, NH, in 2007. ⓟ (Athena1955)

STOPPED FOR LUNCH. IS IT OKAY?! *(bottom left):* This was at the bird feeder on our back patio during an early afternoon. It was nice of him to smile and pose for me. ⓟ (charlieg)

EAGLE ON ROCK FISHING *(bottom right):* A bald eagle on Lake Winnipesaukee. ⓟ Lauren Goldsmith (lgoldsmithma)

HUMMINGBIRD MOTH ON BUTTERFLY BUSH *(top left):* Nottingham, NH. Saw this cool little guy busy on my butterfly bush. ℗ (58healey)

HERE'S LOOKING AT YOU *(right):* ℗ Fred Martin (Weeks)

FALL *(bottom left):* Chippy loves fall. This is one of Bradford, NH's famous residents — well, famous at my house anyway. Chippy is busy getting ready for the long winter, but also taking a little break in the stein. ℗ (potofgold)

ONE DAY IN
10·10·10
NEW HAMPSHIRE

In 2009, we asked everyone in New Hampshire to share pictures of one day in their lives: 9.9.09. It was so successful, we asked viewers if they would share photos of their 10.10.10. Thousands of images poured into our web site. Here are just a few 10.10.10 fall photos received.

GRANITE GOLD MASTER MASON *(left):* Gail M. Timmins (Brewin)

JON HINES 20-YEAR-OLD WHEELIE *(right):* Motorcycle stunting last minute idea for 10-10-10.
(hines57stunts)

ROBARTWOOD POND REFLECTION *(top):* Paddling on Robartwood pond/Campton bog on 10/10/10. (JADougan)

TYLER, 10, IN HIS 10TH YEAR ON 10/10/10 AT 10:10 AM *(bottom left):* Tyler turned 10 this year, and this photo was taken at 10:10 a.m. on 10-10-10! (mjdupuis)

AUSTIN AND NANA ON 10-10-10 *(bottom right):* Weekend with Nana. Backyard Manchester, NH. (Summer9056)

WEDDING *(top):* My daughter's 10-10-10 wedding at 10:10.10 a.m. in Meredith Center at Wicwas Lake Grange #292. ℗ (DoubleD)

GOLFING IN SOMERSWORTH *(bottom left):* We had a 10 a.m. tee time at Sunningdale in Somersworth, NH. In the photo are, from left to right, Owen McLean, age 6, Chuck McLean, age 36, and Jackson McIntyre, age 9. We have the 9th flag showing for Channel 9! ℗ (ChuckMcLean)

PUMPKINS 10-10-10 *(bottom right):* The Remicks having fun carving pumpkins on a great Sunday in Somersworth, NH, on 10-10-10. ℗ (Remick)

LOON LIGHT HOUSE 10-10-10 *(following):* 10-10-10 Last boat ride to see Fall colors on Lake Sunapee. ℗ (Bcooper5)